MERMAID FOOD

MERMAID FOOD

50 DEEP SEA DESSERTS TO INSPIRE YOUR IMAGINATION

CAYLA GALLAGHER

HOST OF THE YouTube COOKING SHOW *PANKOBUNNY*

Racehorse Publishing

Racehorse Publishing books may be purchased in bulk at special discounts for sales promotion, corporate gifts, fund-raising, or educational purposes. Special editions can also be created to specifications. For details, contact the Special Sales Department, Skyhorse Publishing, 307 West 36th Street, 11th Floor, New York, NY 10018 or info@skyhorsepublishing.com.

Racehorse Publishing™ is a pending trademark of Skyhorse Publishing, Inc.®, a Delaware corporation.

Visit our website at www.skyhorsepublishing.com.

10 9 8 7 6 5 4 3 2 1

Library of Congress Cataloging-in-Publication Data

Names: Gallagher, Cayla, author.
Title: Mermaid food: 50 deep sea desserts to inspire your imagination /
    Cayla Gallagher.
Description: New York: Racehorse Publishing, [2019] | Includes
    bibliographical references and index.
Identifiers: LCCN 2019011274 (print) | LCCN 2019011423 (ebook) | ISBN
    9781631584268 (Ebook) | ISBN 9781631584251 (alk. paper)
Subjects: LCSH: Cake. | Cookies. | Desserts. | LCGFT: Cookbooks.
Classification: LCC TX771 (ebook) | LCC TX771 .G346 2019 (print) | DDC
    641.86—dc23
LC record available at https://lccn.loc.gov/2019011274

Cover design by Mona Lin
Cover photo by Cayla Gallagher

Print ISBN: 978-1-63158-425-1
Ebook ISBN: 978-1-63158-426-8

Printed in China

CONTENTS

INTRODUCTION

Welcome to my second cookbook, *Mermaid Food*! This time last year, I was putting the finishing touches on my first book, *Unicorn Food*, and pinching myself that I would soon become an author while still in my twenties—I never would have believed that I would be writing another book just a year later!

After completing and publishing *Unicorn Food*, I had some time to reflect on the process and what I'd change if I had the chance to do it again. I am so incredibly proud of *Mermaid Food* and I really hope that you love it too.

As a little girl, I loved mermaids and any glittery, under-the-sea goodies so I tried to channel my younger self while baking. These treats will be perfect for your little mermaid's birthday party, stormy enough for a Kraken- and pirate-themed event, and yet elegant enough for a beachy bridal shower. Some of my favorites include the KRAKEN KAKE (page 19), OCTOPUS CAKE POPS (page 17), MERMAID MILKSHAKE (page 79), BEACHY RICE CEREAL POPS (page 89), and REEF MALLOWS (page 105).

Several of these recipes also exist as video tutorials on my YouTube channel, *pankobunny*, so I highly suggest checking them out, especially if you'd like a step-by-step tutorial. If you have questions about any recipe in this book, please feel free to DM me on Instagram or YouTube and I will be happy to help you!

Thank you so much for purchasing this book. I hope that it sparks inspiration and sweetness!

—Love,
Cayla

Cakes & Cupcakes

Mermaid Fin Cake

MAKES 1 CAKE

This is a staple at a mermaid party! The fin is made from delicious chocolate and this entire cake can be customized to fit your color theme. Imagine how pretty a hot pink tail would be, or even a zombie mermaid tail!

Cake:
1½ cups unsalted butter, room temperature
3 cups sugar
1½ tsp. vanilla extract
9 eggs, room temperature
4½ cups all-purpose flour
1½ tsp. baking soda
1½ tsp. salt
1¾ cups sour cream
Teal, blue, and purple food coloring

Buttercream:
3 cups unsalted butter, room temperature
1½ tsp. vanilla extract
7 cups confectioner's sugar

Mermaid Fin:
½ cup white candy melts
3 green candy melts
2 yellow candy melts
1 tsp. vodka, or any clear food flavoring
Purple luster dust
Gold luster dust

Bake the cake:
1. Preheat oven to 350°F. Grease and flour 3 (8-inch) round cake pans.

2. Beat the butter and sugar with an electric mixer until pale and fluffy. Add the vanilla extract, then add the eggs one at a time, mixing with each addition.

3. In a separate bowl, combine the flour, baking soda, and salt. Add this to the batter in 2 additions, alternating with the sour cream.

4. Divide the batter between 3 bowls. Dye one each teal, blue, and purple, with just a few drops of food coloring. Pour each of the 3 different shades between your 3 cake pans, then swirl with a knife. Bake 30 minutes, or until a skewer inserted into the cakes comes out clean. Cool in the pans for 10 minutes, then transfer to a wire rack and cool completely. The cakes may deflate slightly after coming out of the oven, but don't worry!

Make the buttercream:
1. Beat the butter with an electric mixer until pale and fluffy. Add the vanilla extract and beat until combined. Add the confectioner's sugar one cup at a time, then beat for 3 to 5 minutes, until fluffy.

Assembly:
1. Slice the tops and bottoms off the cakes to remove any excess browning. Stack the cakes, spreading some buttercream between each layer. Use a serrated knife to carve the cake into a pointed, dome-like shape. Don't worry—you can use the scraps to make cake pops!

2. Coat the entire cake in a thin layer of buttercream. Crumbs may get caught up in the buttercream, but this will prevent them from getting stuck in the final layer of buttercream.

3. Divide the remaining buttercream into 3 bowls and dye one each teal, blue, and purple. Place them into piping bags fitted with large, round piping tips.

continued on next page

4. Working from the top, pipe rows of dollops of buttercream. You can create any pattern you like—you can scatter contrasting colors throughout a row, which is what I did, or scatter all 3 colors throughout the cake. To create the scallop pattern, pipe one row of dollops, then use a rounded spatula to smush the center of the dollop and drag it downwards. Wipe the spatula between each dollop, then continue to the next row. Cover the entire cake in buttercream scallops.

5. To make the fin, combine the white, green, and yellow candy melts in a microwave-safe bowl and microwave at 30-second intervals until fully melted. Draw a fin onto a sheet of parchment paper, making sure to extend the fin downwards, creating an extension that will stick into the cake. Flip over onto a baking sheet, so that the side with the ink is facing down. Spread the candy melts onto the parchment paper, using the drawing as a template. Transfer the baking sheet to the freezer for the candy melts to set, about 20 minutes.

6. Dip a clean paintbrush into vodka, or any clear food coloring, then dip into gold and purple luster dust. Paint this onto the chocolate fin, to create a beautiful sheen. Then stick the fin into the top of the cake and enjoy!

This recipe has a video tutorial! Check out my pankobunny *YouTube channel to see how to make it.*

Seaside Cake

MAKES ONE 6-INCH CAKE

This a "naked" cake, meaning that there is very minimal buttercream on the outside! I love this look because it highlights the ombre cake layers and isn't as heavy as other buttercream-laden cakes. This cake is perfect for a children's party, but also elegant enough to be served at a bridal or baby shower!

Cake:
1 cup unsalted butter, room temperature
2 cups sugar
1 tsp. vanilla extract
6 eggs, room temperature
3 cups all-purpose flour
1 tsp. baking soda
1 tsp. salt
1¼ cups sour cream
Blue food coloring

Buttercream:
1 cup unsalted butter, room temperature
½ tsp. vanilla extract
2½ cups confectioner's sugar
Chocolate Seashell Truffles (page 87)
Brown sugar

Bake the cake:

1. Preheat oven to 350°F. Grease and flour 4 (8-inch) round cake pans.

2. Beat the butter and sugar with an electric mixer until pale and fluffy. Add the vanilla extract, then the eggs one a time, mixing with each addition.

3. In a separate bowl, combine the flour, baking soda, and salt. Add this to the batter in 2 additions, alternating with the sour cream.

4. Divide the batter between 4 bowls. Keep one bowl white and dye the remaining bowls pale, medium, and dark blue, just adding extra drops for a darker color. Pour one color each into your prepared cake pans. Bake for 20 minutes, or until a skewer inserted into the cakes comes out clean. Cool in the pans for 10 minutes, then transfer to a wire rack and cool completely.

Make the buttercream:

1. Beat the butter with an electric mixer until pale and fluffy. Add the vanilla extract and beat until combined. Add the confectioner's sugar one cup at a time, then beat for 3 to 5 minutes, until fluffy.

Assembly:

1. Using a plate as a guide, trim off the edges of all cakes—this will make them look pretty when they are being stacked. Also remove any excess browning from the tops and bottoms of the cakes.

continued on page 7

2. Stack the cakes, starting with the dark blue cake and transitioning to the white cake, spreading a generous amount of buttercream between each layer. Spread the buttercream right to the edges of the cakes. Then spread a thin layer of buttercream on top of the cake.

3. Holding an offset spatula vertically against the surface of the cake, rotate the cake to smooth the buttercream filling.

4. Sprinkle some brown sugar on top of the cake to look like sand. Press some brown sugar into a small glass, like a shot glass, then turn out onto the top of the cake to resemble a sandcastle.

5. Use your Chocolate Seashell Truffles to decorate the cake.

6. Enjoy!

This recipe has a video tutorial! Check out my pankobunny *YouTube channel to see how to make it.*

Mermaid Swiss Roll Cake

MAKES ONE STANDARD SIZE SWISS ROLL CAKE

This style of swiss roll cake is widely popular and actually quite easy! Baking the pattern into the cake removes the need for frosting and allows you to control the sweetness. For an extra special touch, the cake can be decorated with chocolate, extra whipped cream, or drawn on with an edible ink pen.

Pattern:
3 Tbsp. unsalted butter, room temperature
½ cup confectioner's sugar
3 large egg whites
¼ tsp. vanilla extract
⅔ cup all-purpose flour
Green food coloring

Cake Batter:
6 large eggs, yolks and whites separated
Pinch salt
1 cup sugar, divided
2 tsp. vanilla extract
5 Tbsp. unsalted butter, melted and cooled
1 cup all-purpose flour
Blue food coloring

Filling:
1 cup whipping cream, cold
2 Tbsp. confectioner's sugar
1 tsp. vanilla extract

Make the pattern:

1. Beat the butter with an electric mixer until light and fluffy. Add the sugar and beat until combined. Add the egg whites and vanilla extract and beat until combined. Add the flour on low speed. Dye the batter green with a couple drops of food coloring.

2. Place the batter into a piping bag fitted with a small, round piping tip.

3. Line a swiss roll pan with parchment paper. Pipe scallops all over the paper.

4. Transfer the pan to the freezer and freeze for 30 minutes.

Make the cake batter:

1. Preheat oven to 350°F.

2. Beat the 6 egg whites and a pinch of salt with an electric mixer until soft peaks form. Add half of the sugar and beat until stiff, glossy peaks are formed.

3. In a separate bowl, beat the egg yolks and remaining sugar with an electric mixer until pale and doubled in volume. Gradually add the vanilla extract and butter and mix until well combined.

4. Add the flour to the batter in 2 additions, alternating with the egg whites. Dye the batter pale blue and gently fold to combine.

continued on next page

5. Pour the batter into the swiss roll cake pan, on top of the pattern. Gently smooth the surface and bake for 13 to 15 minutes, until the edges are golden.

6. Dust a large sheet of wax paper with confectioner's sugar. As soon as the cake comes out of the oven, invert it onto the wax paper. Peel off the top layer of parchment paper, place another layer of wax paper on top, then invert again, so that the patterned side is facing down. Remove the wax paper and starting at one long end, gently roll the cake up. Wrap in a kitchen towel and cool completely.

Make the filling:

1. Beat the whipping cream with an electric mixer until soft peaks form. Add the confectioner's sugar and vanilla extract and beat until stiff peaks form.

Assembly:

1. Gently unroll the cake and peel off the wax paper. Spread the filling onto the surface and roll the cake back up again.

2. Wrap the cake in plastic wrap and chill in the fridge for 4 hours, or up to overnight.

3. Slice off the ends to create a clean look and enjoy!

Mermaid Mousse Cake

MAKES ONE 9-INCH CAKE

This is a delicate and creamy white chocolate mousse cake with a dark chocolate cake base. I think it's beautiful and elegant and looks just like the sea!

Cake Base:

⅓ cup all-purpose flour

⅓ cup sugar

3 Tbsp. cocoa powder

¼ tsp. baking powder

¼ tsp. baking soda

Pinch salt

½ large egg, beaten

2 Tbsp. milk

1½ Tbsp. oil

¼ tsp. vanilla extract

2 Tbsp. water

Mousse:

6 tsp. gelatin

9 Tbsp. cold water

10 egg whites

3⅓ cups whipping cream

1½ tsp. vanilla extract

1 cup milk

4½ cups white chocolate (a chocolate bar will work best)

Blue food coloring

Chocolate Seashell Truffles (page 87)

Blue sanding sugar

White sprinkles

White pearl-like candies

Pink jelly beans

Bake the cake base:

1. Preheat oven to 350°F.

2. Place the flour, sugar, cocoa powder, baking powder, baking soda, and salt in the bowl of an electric mixer and mix on low speed until fully combined. Add the egg, milk, oil, vanilla, and water and mix until smooth.

3. Line the bottom of a 10-inch springform pan with parchment paper and pour the batter into the pan, spreading the batter right to the edges. Bake for 20 to 30 minutes, or until a skewer inserted into the center comes out clean. Place the pan on a cooling rack and cool completely. Remove the cake from the pan and remove the parchment paper lining. Return the cake to the pan and set aside.

Make the mousse:

1. Sprinkle the gelatin into the cold water and set aside. Beat the egg whites until stiff peaks form.

2. In a separate bowl, combine the whipping cream and vanilla extract and beat until soft peaks form. Set both bowls aside.

3. Set a small saucepan to medium heat and add the milk. Just before the milk comes to a boil, turn off the heat and add the gelatin and water mixture. Once the gelatin has fully dissolved, add the white chocolate and whisk until fully melted. You may need to turn the heat back on to fully melt the chocolate.

continued on page 13

4. Add this mixture to the whipped cream and fold to combine (do not use an electric mixer—it will deflate the filling!). Then add the egg whites and fold to combine, making sure to keep the mixture as airy as possible.

5. Add a couple drops of blue food coloring and gently fold it a couple times, creating a marble effect.

6. Pour the mousse into the pan and smooth the surface.

7. Place the cake onto a large tray and place in the fridge to chill overnight. Because the filling is quite liquidy, a little bit may leak out from the edges of the pan. To help this, bunch some paper towel around the base of the pan and keep it on the tray while it's setting in the fridge.

8. Run a warm, damp dishcloth around the sides of the pan, then slide a sharp knife along the inside walls of the pan to help loosen the cake. Gently unlatch the sides of the pan and slide it off the cake.

9. Decorate the cake with blue sanding sugar, white sprinkles, pink jelly beans, Chocolate Seashell Truffles, and pearl-like candies. Slice and enjoy!

This recipe has a video tutorial! Check out my pankobunny *YouTube channel to see how to make it.*

Clownfish Cake

MAKES ONE 9 X 13-INCH CAKE

Clownfish are highly requested fish at mermaid or underwater parties, so this cake is a must! This is so easy to make for bakers at any skill level and you don't need a special cake pan to bake it.

Cake Batter:
1 cup unsalted butter, room temperature
2 cups sugar
3 tsp. vanilla extract
6 large eggs
3 cups all-purpose flour
1 tsp. baking soda
1 tsp. salt
1½ cups sour cream (or milk)

Buttercream:
4 cups unsalted butter, room temperature
2 tsp. vanilla extract, or seeds from 1 vanilla bean
10 cups confectioner's sugar
Black and orange food coloring

Bake the cake:
1. Preheat oven to 350°F. Grease and flour a 9 x 13-inch cake pan.

2. Beat the butter and sugar with an electric mixer until pale and smooth. Add the vanilla extract, then the eggs one at a time, mixing with each addition.

3. In a separate bowl, combine the flour, baking soda, and salt. Add this to the batter in 2 additions, alternating with the sour cream.

4. Spoon the batter into your prepared pan. Bake for 40 to 50 minutes, or until a skewer inserted into the center comes out clean. Cool completely.

Make the buttercream:
1. Beat the butter with an electric mixer until pale and fluffy. Add the vanilla extract and confectioner's sugar one cup at a time, beating with each addition.

2. Divide the buttercream into 3 bowls. Leave one bowl white and dye one orange and one black.

Assembly:
1. Using a serrated knife, slice the top and bottom off the cake to smooth the surface and remove any excess browning. Then slice the cake horizontally into 2 even layers. Stack the layers and carve the cake into a fish shape.

2. Stack the cakes and spread some white buttercream between the layers. Place the orange, black, and remaining white buttercream into piping bags fitted with small, star-shaped piping tips. My favorite is the #28 piping tip.

3. Pipe the black markings onto the cake first, by piping in an upward motion, creating clusters of stars. Follow with the white buttercream, then the orange buttercream. Pipe the eye on last, so that it stands out. Enjoy your cute clownfish!

Octopus Cake Pops

MAKES 12 CAKE POPS

These have got to be my favorite treats in this book! Their expressions make me laugh so much! I purposely haven't specified the cake or buttercream recipe here, because you can use whatever you like! My favorite cake and buttercream for cake pops is my vanilla cake recipe, which is featured in the Narwhal Cake (page 35). Looking for a chocolate cake instead? Check out the Kraken Kake (page 19)!

Ingredients:

2½ cups (about 10 oz.) cake crumbs
½ cup buttercream
½ cup fondant, any color
3 cups purple candy melts
12 lollipop sticks
24 candy eyes

Directions:

1. Combine the cake crumbs with the buttercream and mix until everything is well combined and the cake can be molded into shapes. Roll it into 12 balls and place on a plate lined with plastic wrap.

2. Divide the fondant into 12 pieces and shape them into flat stars. Press them onto the bottom of each cake pop. Freeze the cake pops for 30 minutes, or until firm.

3. Reshape the cake pops into smoother circles. If they have significantly softened, return them to the fridge while you melt the candy melts.

4. To melt the candy melts, place them in a microwave safe bowl and microwave for 30-second intervals until melted, stirring at each interval.

5. Dip a lollipop stick into the candy melts and insert them into the top of the cake pops. Return the cake pops to the freezer until the candy melts have set.

6. Dip the top of each candy eye into the candy melts to create eyelids. Place them on a tray and set aside.

7. Dunk each cake pop into the candy melts and allow the excess to drip off the bottom. Immediately stick 2 candy eyes onto the octopus and return the cake pop to the plastic wrap-lined plate. Repeat with the remaining cake pops, then place in the fridge for a final set, about 30 minutes.

Kraken Kake

MAKES ONE 6-INCH CAKE

The Kraken is breaking out of this cake and thrashing around in stormy buttercream seas! This cake is the BEST chocolate cake you will ever make. It is so incredibly moist, chocolatey, and addictive. You won't be able to stop at one slice!

Cake Batter:
2 cups all-purpose flour
2 cups sugar
¾ cup cocoa powder
2 tsp. baking powder
1½ tsp. baking soda
1 tsp. salt
1 cup milk
½ cup vegetable oil
2 large eggs
2 tsp. vanilla extract
1 cup boiling water

Buttercream:
4 cups unsalted butter, room temperature
2 tsp. vanilla extract, or seeds from 1 vanilla bean
10 cups confectioner's sugar
Black and blue food coloring

Tentacles:
1 cup black fondant
3 lollipop sticks or bamboo skewers

Bake the cake:
1. Preheat oven to 350°F. Grease and flour 4 (6-inch) round cake pans.

2. Place the flour, sugar, cocoa powder, baking powder, baking soda, and salt in a large bowl and mix together.

3. Add the milk, vegetable oil, eggs, and vanilla extract and mix with an electric mixer until combined.

4. Slowly add the boiling water and mix until well combined.

5. Divide the batter evenly between the pans and bake for 30 to 35 minutes, until a skewer inserted into the centers comes out clean. Cool for 15 minutes in the pans, then turn onto a wire rack and cool completely.

Make the buttercream:
1. Beat the butter with an electric mixer until pale and fluffy. Add the vanilla extract and confectioner's sugar one cup at a time, beating with each addition.

2. Dye the buttercream pale blue.

Make the tentacles:
1. Divide the fondant into 3 pieces in a variety of sizes. Then remove a little bit of each piece. These will be for the suction cups.

continued on next page

2. Shape the larger pieces of fondant into tentacles. Roll the smaller pieces of fondant into long sausages, then shape into rings. Dab some water onto the tentacles and attach the rings. Water acts like a glue for fondant!

3. Set the tentacles aside on a plate lined with plastic wrap. If you are sticking a tentacle onto the sides of the cake, stick some bamboo skewers into the base of the tentacle. These tentacles can be made a few days in advance, if desired. Continue with the rest of the cake.

Assembly:

1. Slice the tops and bottoms off the cakes to smooth the surface and remove any excess browning.

2. Stack the cakes and spread some buttercream between each layer.

3. Coat the cake in a thin layer of buttercream, called a crumb coat. This will catch any excess cake crumbs. Chill the cake in the fridge for 20 minutes.

4. Divide the buttercream into 4 bowls. Use more blue and black food coloring to give the buttercream an ombre effect, leaving one bowl light blue and dyeing the remaining 3 to make them progressively darker. I added a couple drops of black food coloring, along with the blue food coloring, to the last 2 bowls, to give them a murky, dark sea water effect.

5. Place all the buttercream into individual piping bags fitted with a large, angled piping tip. I like the #127 tip.

6. Start with the darkest shade of buttercream. Hold the piping bag horizontally to the cake so that the wider end of the piping tip is against the cake and the narrow end is not touching the cake. Pipe the buttercream, starting at the base of the cake, in a horizontal line. As you pipe, wiggle the bag vertically, creating wavy patterns. Continue working your way up the cake, until it is ¼ covered. Switch to the next lighter shade, continue another ¼ of the cake, then use the next lighter shade, and so on.

7. Once all sides of the cake have been covered, continue piping the lightest buttercream on the top of the cake by piping a spiral instead of stripes, starting from the center of the cake and working outwards.

8. Stick the tentacles onto the cake and enjoy!

This recipe has a video tutorial! Check out my pankobunny *YouTube channel to see how to make it.*

Underwater Cake

MAKES ONE 6-INCH CAKE

This is the ultimate mermaid cake! The cutest little mermaid sits among sweet, chocolatey sea creatures and even has a fin made from cake pops! You can find dolls without legs at baking supply stores to use as the mermaid, so no need to worry about trying to fit the legs somewhere in the cake. Decorate and slice with ease!

Cake Batter:
1 cup unsalted butter, room temperature
2 cups sugar
3 tsp. vanilla extract
6 large eggs
3 cups all-purpose flour
1 tsp. baking soda
1 tsp. salt
1½ cups sour cream (or milk)

Buttercream:
2 cups unsalted butter, room temperature
1 tsp. vanilla extract, or seeds from 1 vanilla bean
5 cups confectioner's sugar
Blue, green, and purple food coloring
Isomalt coral (Coral Reef Cupcakes, page 25)
Chocolate Seashell Truffles (page 87)
Candy rocks
Colorful candies
Barbie doll top (without legs)

Bake the cake:
1. Preheat oven to 350°F. Grease and flour 4 (6-inch) round cake pans.

2. Beat the butter and sugar with an electric mixer until pale and smooth. Add the vanilla extract, then add the eggs one at a time, mixing with each addition.

3. In a separate bowl, combine the flour, baking soda, and salt. Add this to the batter in 2 additions, alternating with the sour cream.

4. Spoon the batter into your prepared baking pans. Bake for 30 minutes, or until a skewer inserted into the centers comes out clean. Cool completely.

Make the buttercream:
1. Beat the butter with an electric mixer until pale and fluffy. Add the vanilla extract, then add the confectioner's sugar one cup at a time, beating with each addition.

2. Dye the buttercream pale blue. Dye ¼ cup of the blue buttercream green, and dye another ¼ cup purple. Place the green buttercream in a piping bag fitted with a small, angled piping tip (#102). Place 1 tablespoon of the purple buttercream into a piping bag fitted with a small, round piping tip, and the remaining buttercream into a piping bag fitted with a small, star-shaped piping tip (#30).

continued on page 23

Assembly:

1. Slice the tops and bottoms off the cakes to smooth the surface and remove any excess browning. Keep the cake scraps! Stack the cakes and spread some blue buttercream between each layer. Cover the entire cake in a thin layer of buttercream and place in the fridge to chill.

2. Crumble the cake scraps into fine pieces. Add a couple dollops of buttercream and mix until the cake sticks together and can be molded into a shape. Mold it into what will become the mermaid's tail, creating a curve at the end to allow it to sit comfortably on the cake. Place the tail in the fridge to chill and stiffen.

3. Cover the cake in a thick, generous layer of buttercream. Press some candy rocks onto the base of the cake. Place the remaining blue buttercream into a piping bag and snip off the end to create a large, round piping tip. Pipe dollops where you plan to stick candy and decorations. This will act as glue, keeping everything in place and propped up.

4. Place the mermaid tail on top of the cake and stick the Barbie doll top on top. Use the green buttercream to pipe scallops onto the tail, starting at the tip of the tail and working towards the body. To make the scallop shape, position the piping tip so that the narrow opening is against the tail and pipe little "u" shapes repeatedly. Cover the entire tail.

5. Pipe the bikini with the purple buttercream. Use the remaining purple buttercream to pipe little barnacles around the sides of the cake. Decorate the cake with Isomalt Coral, Chocolate Seashell Truffles, sprinkles, and mermaid-colored candy.

6. The blank space on the side of the cake can be used as space to pipe a name, or "Happy Birthday!"

Coral Reef Cupcakes

MAKES 12 CUPCAKES

To create this gorgeous, vibrant pink coral, we're using isomalt, a form of artificial sweetener derived from beets It's much easier to use than traditional hard candy and can be found easily online. You'll need a candy thermometer, which might sound like a pain, but opens so many sugar-making doors once you invest in one! Choose a vibrant cupcake liner to make them even more stunning!

Cupcake Batter:
½ cup unsalted butter, room temperature
1 cup sugar
1½ tsp. vanilla extract
3 large eggs
1½ cups all-purpose flour
½ tsp. baking soda
½ tsp. salt
¾ cups sour cream (or milk)

Buttercream:
2 cups unsalted butter, room temperature
1 tsp. vanilla extract, or seeds from 1 vanilla bean
5 cups confectioner's sugar

Coral:
4 cups isomalt crystals
1 cup water
Liquid food coloring
10 cups of ice

Bake the cupcakes:
1. Preheat oven to 350°F. Prepare a cupcake pan with colorful liners.

2. Beat the butter and sugar with an electric mixer until pale and smooth. Add the vanilla extract, then add the eggs one at a time, mixing with each addition.

3. In a separate bowl, combine the flour, baking soda, and salt. Add this to the batter in 2 additions, alternating with the sour cream.

4. Spoon the batter into a lined cupcake pan. Bake for 15 to 20 minutes, or until a skewer inserted into the centers comes out clean. Cool completely.

Make the buttercream:
1. Beat the butter with an electric mixer until pale and fluffy. Add the vanilla extract, then add the confectioner's sugar one cup at a time, beating with each addition.

2. Place the buttercream into a piping bag and snip off the end to create a large opening. Alternatively, you could use a large, round piping tip.

Make the coral:
1. Pour the isomalt crystals and water into a heavy saucepan. Set to medium heat and whisk until dissolved.

continued on next page

2. Attach a candy thermometer and heat to 280°F. Add the food coloring, stir, then continue heating to 320°F. If sugar crystals form on the sides of the pan, dip a pastry brush in water and brush it onto the sides.

3. Once the isomalt reaches 320°F, remove it from the heat and pour the isomalt into a heatproof bowl. I used an aluminum mixing bowl. Allow it to cool until it gets thicker and resembles thick honey.

4. Fill a deep bowl with the ice. Drizzle the isomalt onto the ice. As it trickles down through the ice, it will mold to the curves of the ice cubes. Pour 2–3 layers in each spot, to ensure the isomalt is thick and won't break.

5. Allow the isomalt to fully cool, then break it into pieces with your hands. It can be sharp, so be careful! Place the isomalt on a plate lined with plastic wrap and set aside.

Assembly:
1. Pipe a swirl of buttercream onto each cupcake. Top with a piece of isomalt and enjoy!

This recipe has a video tutorial! Check out my pankobunny *YouTube channel to see how to make it.*

Mermaid Number Birthday Cake

MAKES ONE 9 X 13-INCH CAKE, ENOUGH FOR 1 DIGIT

This is a show-stopping way to celebrate a little mermaid's birthday! This recipe can be doubled to accommodate for double digits. Decorate with chocolate or your mermaid's favorite candies!

Cake Batter:
1 cup unsalted butter, room temperature
2 cups sugar
3 tsp. vanilla extract
6 large eggs
3 cups all-purpose flour
1 tsp. baking soda
1 tsp. salt
1½ cups sour cream (or milk)

Buttercream:
2 cups unsalted butter, room temperature
1 tsp. vanilla extract, or seeds from 1 vanilla bean
5 cups confectioner's sugar
Blue food coloring
Chocolate Mermaid Tails (page 109)
Chocolate Seaside Truffles (page 87)
Mermaid-colored sprinkles

Bake the cake:

1. Preheat oven to 350°F. Grease and flour a 9 x 13-inch baking pan.

2. Beat the butter and sugar with an electric mixer until pale and smooth. Add the vanilla extract, then add the eggs one at a time, mixing with each addition.

3. In a separate bowl, combine the flour, baking soda, and salt. Add this to the batter in 2 additions, alternating with the sour cream.

4. Spoon the batter into your prepared baking pan. Bake for 40 to 50 minutes, or until a skewer inserted into the center comes out clean. Cool completely.

Make the buttercream:

1. Beat the butter with an electric mixer until pale and fluffy. Add the vanilla extract, then add the confectioner's sugar one cup at a time, beating with each addition.

2. Divide into two, dye half the buttercream pale blue, and leave the remaining half white.

3. Place the buttercream into piping bags. Snip off the ends about 1 to 2 inches from the tip, creating large, round piping tips. Alternatively, you could attach 2 large, round piping tips.

continued on page 29

Assembly:

1. Slice the top off the cake to create a flat, smooth surface and remove any browning. Slices the sides off the cake as well, removing any remaining browning. Slice the cake horizontally into 2 even layers, then stack them on top of each other. Carve the cake into your desired number. If you want to sketch the number on the cake first, you can use a little bit of buttercream or an edible ink pen.

2. Remove the top layer and pipe dollops of white buttercream onto the bottom layer. As you pipe each dollop, drag the piping tip downwards, creating an indent in the dollop. Pipe 2 to 3 rows of dollops along the entire layer, then place the other cake layer on top. Repeat the same piping technique, but use the blue buttercream.

3. Decorate with Chocolate Mermaid Tails, Seaside Chocolate Truffles, and sprinkles.

Mermaid Cupcakes

MAKES 12 CUPCAKES

These cupcakes are show-stoppers! They have two (!!) layers of buttercream, are covered in sparkly sprinkles, and topped with a delicious chocolate mermaid tail. They would be perfect on their own, served with tea or coffee, or alongside my Underwater Cake (page 21) or Mermaid Fin Cake (page 3).

Cupcake Batter:
½ cup unsalted butter, room temperature
1 cup sugar
½ tsp. vanilla extract
3 eggs, room temperature
1½ cups all-purpose flour
½ tsp. baking soda
½ tsp. salt
¾ cup buttermilk
Pink, blue, and purple food coloring

Buttercream:
2 cups unsalted butter, room temperature
1 tsp. vanilla extract
5 cups confectioner's sugar
Blue food coloring
Chocolate Mermaid Tails (page 109)
Pink, gold, and silver sprinkles
Silver star sprinkles

Bake the cupcakes:
1. Preheat oven to 350°F. Prepare a muffin pan with liners.

2. Beat the butter and sugar with an electric mixer until pale and fluffy. Add the vanilla extract, then add the eggs one a time, mixing with each addition.

3. In a separate bowl, combine the flour, baking soda, and salt. Add this to the batter in 2 additions, alternating with the buttermilk. Divide the batter into 3 bowls and dye one each pink, blue, and purple.

4. Pour a bit of each shade of batter into your prepared muffin tin. Bake for 20 minutes, or until a skewer inserted into the cupcakes comes out clean. Cool in the pan for 10 minutes, then transfer to a wire rack and cool completely.

Make the buttercream:
1. Beat the butter with an electric mixer until pale and fluffy. Add the vanilla extract and beat until combined. Add the confectioner's sugar one cup at a time, then beat for 3 to 5 minutes, until fluffy. Dye the buttercream pale blue.

2. Divide the buttercream in half. Place half in a piping bag fitted with a large, round piping tip. Place the other half in a piping bag fitted with a large, star-shaped piping tip.

Assembly:
1. Combine the pink, gold, and silver sprinkles in a bowl.

2. Pipe a ring of buttercream on top of each cupcake with the round piping tip. Dunk the cupcakes into the sprinkles, fully coating the buttercream. Pipe another swirl of buttercream with the star-shaped piping tip and top with silver star sprinkles. Top with a Chocolate Mermaid Fin. Enjoy!

This recipe has a video tutorial! Check out my pankobunny *YouTube channel to see how to make it.*

SHARK TRUFFLES

MAKES 20 TRUFFLES

These sweet little sharks are filled with cake pop mixture! My friends are always shocked when they try these because the smooth creamy filling pairs so well with the delicious chocolatey coating. Use these as decorations for a cake or pack them into a truffle box for the cutest gift imaginable!

Ingredients:

½ cup unsalted butter, room temperature
1 cup sugar
½ tsp. vanilla extract
3 eggs, room temperature
1½ cups all-purpose flour
½ tsp. baking soda
½ tsp. salt
¾ cup sour cream
2 cups vanilla frosting (page 31)
5 cups white candy melts
⅓ cup black candy melts
¼ cup vegetable shortening, melted
40 mini chocolate chips

Make the filling:

1. Preheat oven to 350°F. Prepare a muffin pan with liners.

2. Beat the butter and sugar with an electric mixer until light and fluffy. Add the vanilla extract and eggs and beat until combined. In a separate bowl, combine the flour, baking soda, and salt. Add the flour mixture in 2 additions, alternating with the sour cream.

3. Spoon the mixture into your prepared muffin tin. Bake for 20 minutes, or until a skewer inserted into the cupcakes comes out clean. Cool completely.

4. Crumble the cupcakes into a fine crumb. Add the vanilla frosting and mix well—the mixture should be sticky and easily molded into shapes.

Assembly:

1. Divide the mixture into 20 balls, then gently shape into the shark's body, similar to a teardrop shape. Using a sharp knife, slice 1 cup of white candy melts into long, pointed pieces. You will need 5 pieces per truffle.

2. Stick one piece into the top of the truffles for the classic shark fin, two into the sides as the side fins, then two into the back as the tail.

3. Place the truffles onto a small baking sheet lined with plastic wrap and place in the freezer for 30 minutes, or until firm.

continued on next page

4. Combine the remaining white and black candy melts in a bowl—the addition of a few black candy melts will make it grey! Microwave the candy melts for 30 second intervals, or until fully melted. Add the melted vegetable shortening and mix until combined. This will give the candy melts a thinner consistency and it will coat the truffles much more evenly. Allow the candy melts to slightly cool, until the mixture is just warm.

5. Hold your truffle with a fork and lower into the candy melts, fully coating it. Tap the fork on the side of the bowl to remove any excess candy melts, then return the truffle to the baking sheet.

6. Immediately stick 2 mini chocolate chips onto the truffle as the eyes—this should be done before the candy melts have set, so you will need to move quickly and do this after dunking each truffle.

7. Repeat with the remaining truffles, then transfer the baking sheet to the freezer so the candy melts can fully harden, about 15 minutes. Enjoy!

This recipe has a video tutorial! Check out my pankobunny *YouTube channel to see how to make it.*

Narwhal Cake

MAKES ONE 6-INCH CAKE

Narwhals are the cutest, most amusing little creatures! They are the unicorns of the sea and an absolute must in a mermaid party. This cake is so simple to make and is perfect for beginners! We are using my favorite vanilla cake recipe, which is so moist and fragrant, and topping it with the lightest, fluffiest vanilla buttercream. This cake will not disappoint!

Cake Batter:
1 cup unsalted butter, room temperature
2 cups sugar
3 tsp. vanilla extract
6 large eggs
3 cups all-purpose flour
1 tsp. baking soda
1 tsp. salt
1½ cups sour cream (or milk)

Buttercream:
2 cups unsalted butter, room temperature
1 tsp. vanilla extract, or seeds from
    1 vanilla bean
5 cups confectioner's sugar
Blue food coloring
Black food coloring
⅓ cup white fondant
1 disposable chopstick
2 pink candy melts

Bake the cake:
1. Preheat oven to 350°F. Grease and flour 3 (6-inch) round cake pans.

2. Beat the butter and sugar with an electric mixer until pale and smooth. Add the vanilla extract, then add the eggs one at a time, mixing with each addition.

3. In a separate bowl, combine the flour, baking soda, and salt. Add this to the batter in 2 additions, alternating with the sour cream.

4. Spoon the batter into your prepared baking pans. Bake for 30 minutes, or until a skewer inserted into the centers comes out clean. Cool completely.

Make the buttercream:
1. Beat the butter with an electric mixer until pale and fluffy. Add the vanilla extract, then add the confectioner's sugar one cup at a time, beating with each addition.

2. Dye the buttercream pale blue. Remove about ¼ cup of the buttercream and dye it black. Place the black buttercream into a piping bag fitted with a small, round piping tip.

continued on page 37

Assembly:

1. First, make the horn. Divide the fondant in half and roll it into long sausages. Place the sausages next to each other and wrap them together around the chopstick. Pinch them together at the top and gently squeeze to secure them to the chopstick. Place the horn on a plate lined with plastic wrap and allow it to dry out while you decorate the cake.

2. Slice the bottoms off all cakes, removing any excess browning. Slice the tops off 2 of the cakes, leaving one cake rounded on top. Stack all layers, with the round layer on top. Carve the cake into a tall oval shape with a serrated knife. Spread some blue buttercream between each layer.

3. Coat the entire cake in a thin layer of buttercream. This is called a crumb coat and will help to trap any excess cake crumbs in this thin buttercream layer. Place the cake in the fridge for 20 minutes, to allow the crumb coat to stiffen.

4. Coat the cake in a thick, generous layer of blue buttercream. Draw the narwhal's eyes and mouth with the black buttercream. Stick the pink candy melts onto the cake as blushing cheeks.

5. Place the remaining blue buttercream into a piping bag and snip off the end to create a large, round tip. Create the fins by piping a large dollop on either side of the cake, then dragging the downwards in a flicking motion. Repeat for the tail at the back of the cake.

6. Stick the horn into the forehead area and you're done!

This recipe has a video tutorial! Check out my pankobunny *YouTube channel to see how to make it.*

Shark Pool Cheesecake

MAKES ONE 8-INCH CHEESECAKE

This no-bake cheesecake recipe is my favorite. It is so incredibly creamy, you'll be tempted to eat the entire cake yourself. No kidding. I've mixed some blueberry jam into the batter, but you can absolutely omit the jam or add another flavor of your choice. It is topped with a beautiful blue jelly, resembling a deep shark pool. I love adding jelly layers to my cheesecake to add an extra, luxurious touch to them. And of course— the sharks need somewhere to swim!

Cheesecake Base:
5 Tbsp. unsalted butter, melted
2⅓ cups graham crackers, crumbled into very small pieces

Cheesecake Filling:
1¾ cups cream cheese, room temperature
6½ Tbsp. sugar
1¾ cups whipping cream
¼ cup lemon juice
½ tsp. vanilla extract
5 Tbsp. blueberry jam
Blue food coloring
2 tsp. powdered gelatin
2½ Tbsp. water

Topping:
1 Tbsp. powdered gelatin
½ cup + 1 cup water
2 Tbsp. sugar
1 Tbsp. blueberry jam
Gummy sharks

Make the base:
1. First, make the base of the cheesecake. Mix together the melted butter and crumbled graham crackers, then press them into the bottom of an 8-inch springform pan. Then place this in the fridge while you make the filling.

Make the filling:
1. To make the filling, place the cream cheese in a bowl and beat with an electric mixer until smooth. Add the sugar and combine. Then add the whipping cream, lemon juice, vanilla extract, and blueberry jam and mix until smooth. Add the blue food coloring and dye it your desired shade of blue. Mix together the gelatin and water in a small bowl and microwave for 30 seconds. Add the gelatin to the filling, and mix together with an electric mixer until fully combined.

2. Pour the filling into the cake pan and return it to the fridge to chill until set (approx. 3 hours).

Make the topping:
1. To make the jelly topping, combine the gelatin and ½ cup water in a small bowl, and mix together. Allow to develop for 5 minutes. Pour 1 cup water, sugar, and blueberry jam into a small pot over medium heat. Add the gelatin to the pot, and mix well. Strain the mixture to remove the blueberry pieces from the jam—we only want the blueberry flavor! Allow the mixture to cool for about 10 to 15 minutes, then gently pour half of the jelly onto the top of the cheesecake.

continued on next page

2. Return the cheesecake to the fridge and chill until the jelly has set (approximately 30 to 45 minutes). Decorate the top of the cheesecake with shark gummies, then pour the remaining jelly on top. This will make it look like the gummies are swimming IN the jelly! Return the cheesecake to the fridge to finish setting, for about 1 hour.

3. Carefully remove the cake from the springform pan by running a sharp knife around the edges of the cake, then release the sides of the pan and carefully slide off the cake. This is to ensure that the jelly topping stays intact and doesn't tear. Enjoy!

This recipe has a video tutorial! Check out my pankobunny *YouTube channel to see how to make it.*

Pull-Apart Mermaid Fin Cupcakes

MAKES 24 CUPCAKES

This is the perfect treat for a large party! Simply place this in the center of your festivities and let your guests grab their own cupcake. If you're in a time crunch, this is much quicker than a cake and nobody will be able to tell!

Cupcake Batter:
1 cup unsalted butter, room temperature
2 cups sugar
3 tsp. vanilla extract
6 large eggs
3 cups all-purpose flour
1 tsp. baking soda
1 tsp. salt
1½ cups sour cream (or milk)

Buttercream:
4 cups unsalted butter, room temperature
2 tsp. vanilla extract, or seeds from 1 vanilla bean
10 cups confectioner's sugar
Pink, blue, and purple food coloring
Silver edible glitter

Bake the cupcakes:

1. Preheat oven to 350°F. Prepare 2 cupcake pans with liners.

2. Beat the butter and sugar with an electric mixer until pale and smooth. Add the vanilla extract, then add the eggs one at a time, mixing with each addition.

3. In a separate bowl, combine the flour, baking soda, and salt. Add this to the batter in 2 additions, alternating with the sour cream.

4. Spoon the batter into your prepared pans. Bake for 15 to 20 minutes, or until a skewer inserted into the centers comes out clean. Cool completely.

Make the buttercream:

1. Beat the butter with an electric mixer until pale and fluffy. Add the vanilla extract, then add the confectioner's sugar one cup at a time, beating with each addition.

2. Divide the buttercream into 3 bowls and dye one each blue, purple, and pink.

Assembly:

1. Arrange the cupcakes on a serving tray of your choice. This is important, as it will be quite difficult to move them after decorating!

continued on page 43

2. Place a ⅓ cup-sized dollop of buttercream on top of each cupcake. Start with blue at the top of the fin, purple in the middle, and pink at the tail. Use an offset spatula to smooth the buttercream over each cupcake and connect the buttercream dollops together. Don't worry about creating the ombre effect yet.

3. To create the ombre effect, gently blend just the surface of the purple buttercream up into the blue buttercream and blend the blue buttercream downwards. Repeat with the border between the pink and purple buttercream.

4. Place the remaining pink buttercream into a piping bag and snip off the end, creating a medium-sized round piping tip. Pipe a border around the cupcakes, as well as fish scales and detail on the fin.

5. Sprinkle some edible glitter on top, making the fin sparkle! Make sure to use the glitter last—the piping detail may not stick if piped on after the glitter.

Sandcastle Cake

SERVES UP TO 20 PEOPLE

A must-have for a mermaid party! This cake is quite big and can serve quite a large crowd. It also acts as a beautiful centerpiece for a table filled with sweet, seaside treats.

Cake Batter:
2 cups unsalted butter, room temperature
4 cups sugar
6 tsp. vanilla extract
12 large eggs
6 cups all-purpose flour
2 tsp. baking soda
2 tsp. salt
3 cups sour cream (or milk)

Buttercream:
3 cups unsalted butter, room temperature
1½ tsp. vanilla extract, or seeds from
   1 vanilla bean
7 cups confectioner's sugar
3 cups Edible Sand (page 97)
Chocolate Seashell Truffles (page 87)

Bake the cake:

1. Preheat oven to 350°F. Grease and flour 2 (6-inch) round cake pans, and 2 (9-inch) round cake pans.

2. Beat the butter and sugar with an electric mixer until pale and smooth. Add the vanilla extract, then add the eggs one at a time, mixing with each addition.

3. In a separate bowl, combine the flour, baking soda, and salt. Add this to the batter in 2 additions, alternating with the sour cream.

4. Spoon the batter into your prepared pans. Bake for 30 to 40 minutes, or until a skewer inserted into the centers comes out clean. Cool completely.

Make the buttercream:

1. Beat the butter with an electric mixer until pale and fluffy. Add the vanilla extract, then add the confectioner's sugar one cup at a time, beating with each addition.

Assembly:

1. Slice the tops and bottoms off all the cakes to remove any excess browning and flatten the surfaces. Stack the two large cakes and spread some buttercream in between. Repeat with the two small cakes, but stack them separately from the larger cakes.

2. Coat all cakes in a generous layer of buttercream. Use your hand to press edible sand to the entire surface of all of the cakes.

3. Slide a cake spatula underneath the smaller cake and place it on top of the larger cake.

4. Mix the remaining buttercream with a couple spoons of edible sand. Place it into a piping bag and snip off the end to create a large piping tip. Pipe swirls onto the top of the cake. The sand will make it slightly tricky for them to stick to the cake, but it will work! Sprinkle some more sand on top. Decorate with some Chocolate Seashell Truffles and enjoy!

Baked Goods

Mermaid Macarons

MAKES 10 MACARONS

A bit of a confession here: macarons are not my favorite. Except for this recipe. The texture of these macarons is an absolute dream. The shell gives way to a wonderful, almondy center, which is perfectly balanced by the tartness of the jam. If this is your first time making macarons, don't worry! I've gone into detail step-by-step and I promise that these will work! It took me two attempts and now my macarons are perfect every time.

Ingredients:

1 cup confectioner's sugar
¾ cup almond flour (not almond meal)
2 large egg whites
Pinch cream of tartar
¼ cup superfine sugar
1 tsp. vanilla extract
Blue, pink, red, orange, purple, and brown
    food coloring
Jam, for filling
Edible ink pens

Directions:

1. Combine the confectioner's sugar and almond flour in a bowl, then sift 3 times.

2. Place the egg whites in a large bowl and beat with an electric mixer until foamy. Add the cream of tartar, then beat until soft peaks form. Add the superfine sugar and beat on high speed until stiff peaks form. Add the vanilla extract and gently mix to combine. Sift the dry mixture into the egg mixture and gently fold to combine.

3. Divide the batter into 3 bowls. Dye one bowl blue. Divide the second bowl in half, leaving one half beige and dye the other half brown. The remaining bowl of batter will be used for the hair and the bikinis, so divide it into as many bowls as needed to dye it your desired colors. We used pink for the bikinis, and red, orange, and purple for the hair.

4. Place the batter into piping bags fitted with medium-small sized round tips. First, using the beige or brown batter, pipe the faces and bodies. Use the blue batter to pipe the tails. Use the beige or brown batter to pipe the arms. Pipe the hair with your desired colors, then the bikinis. Tap the baking sheets on your countertop a couple times to remove any air bubbles. Let the macarons sit at room temperature for 30 minutes.

5. Set your oven to 375°F, heat for 5 minutes, then reduce the heat to 325°F. Bake the macarons, one sheet at a time, for 6 to 8 minutes, rotating halfway through. After each batch, increase the heat to 375°F, heat for 5 minutes, then reduce to 325°F and pop the next sheet into the oven.

6. Allow the macarons to cool on the sheet for 2 to 3 minutes, then transfer to a wire rack to fully cool. (I recommend leaving them overnight, since they will be quite delicate and need to slightly stiffen in order to draw the faces.)

7. Draw the facial features with edible ink pens.

8. Place a dollop of raspberry jam between the top and bottom macarons, sandwich them together, and enjoy!

This recipe has a video tutorial! Check out my pankobunny YouTube channel to see how to make it.

Mermaid Doughnuts

MAKES 6 DOUGHNUTS

I love baked doughnuts and this recipe is to die for! They bake in under 10 minutes and are the lightest, most pillowy doughnuts you'll ever try. No dense doughnuts here! We are using my favorite glaze recipe that I always want to eat straight out of the bowl. Try these lovelies—you won't regret it!

Doughnut Batter:

1 cup all-purpose flour
1 tsp. baking powder
¼ tsp. salt
3 Tbsp. unsalted butter, melted
¼ cup sugar
2 Tbsp. honey
1 large egg
1 tsp. vanilla extract
⅓ cup + 1 Tbsp. buttermilk

Glaze:

3 Tbsp. whipping cream
½ cup confectioner's sugar
Drop of vanilla extract
Blue, pink, and purple food coloring
Brown sugar
Pearl-like gum balls or candies
Silver star sprinkles
Chocolate Seashell Truffles (page 87)

Directions:

1. Preheat oven to 400°F. Grease a doughnut pan.

2. Whisk together the flour, baking powder, and salt in a small bowl and set aside. In a large bowl, combine the butter, sugar, honey, egg, and vanilla extract. Add the buttermilk and mix until combined. Add the dry ingredients and mix until just combined—make sure not to overmix.

3. Spoon the batter into a piping bag, then pipe the batter into your prepared pan and bake for 7 minutes. Cool for 1 minute in the pan, then flip the pan over to remove the doughnuts and cool completely on a wire rack.

4. To make the glaze, whisk together the whipping cream and confectioner's sugar until fully combined. Add a small drop of vanilla extract and mix to combine. Divide the glaze into 3 bowls and dye one each pale blue, pink, and purple. Dollop a bit of each color into a larger bowl.

5. Dunk the doughnuts into the glaze. The marble pattern will continue to change as you dunk more doughnuts. Place them on a wire rack. Sprinkle a tiny bit of brown sugar on top to look like sand and decorate with gum ball "pearls" and silver star sprinkles. Top with the Chocolate Seashell Truffles. Enjoy!

This recipe has a video tutorial! Check out my pankobunny YouTube channel to see how to make it.

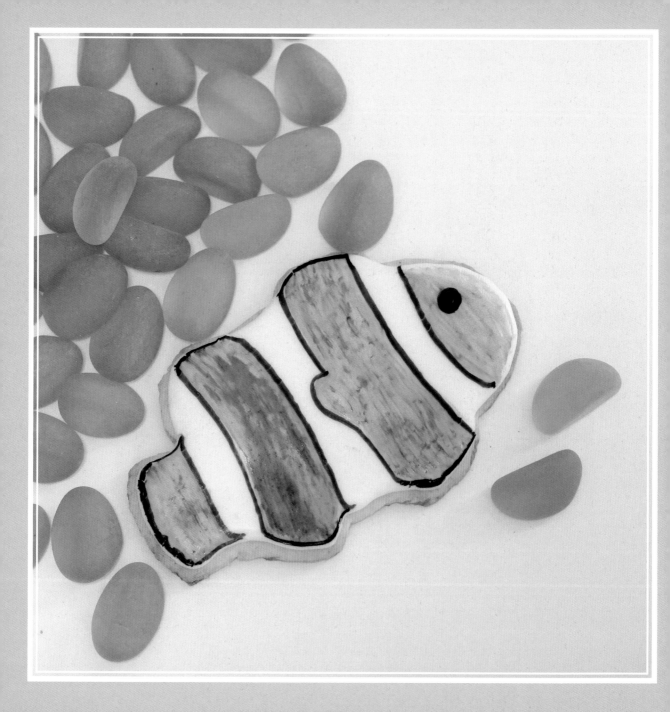

CLOWNFISH COOKIES

MAKES 10-15 COOKIES

Sugar cookie decorating can be intimidating, but this is a fun little trick to make the process much easier! Edible ink pens remove the fuss of fiddling with piping bags and are a perfect beginner's hack. You could even turn this into an activity at a birthday party by giving the guests the white, undecorated fish and challenging them to decorate their own!

Cookie Dough:
2 cups all-purpose flour
¼ tsp. salt
½ tsp. baking powder
½ cup unsalted butter, room temperature
1 cup sugar
2 Tbsp. milk
1 egg
¾ tsp. vanilla extract
1 tsp. fresh lemon zest

Royal Icing:
1 lb confectioner's sugar
5 Tbsp. meringue powder
¼ cup cold water
Edible ink pens

Bake the cookies:

1. Preheat oven to 350°F. Prepare a baking sheet lined with parchment paper.

2. Mix together the flour, salt, and baking powder in a bowl. In a separate bowl, cream the butter and sugar with an electric mixer until it becomes light and fluffy. Add the milk, egg, vanilla, and lemon zest, and mix well. Then slowly add the flour mixture until it is just combined.

3. Shape the dough into a ball, wrap it in plastic wrap, and place in the refrigerator for 1 hour.

4. Lightly dust some flour onto your countertop, and roll the dough out until it is ¼-inch thick. Use a fish-shaped cookie cutter to cut out cookies. Place them on your prepared baking sheet, and bake for about 10 minutes, until lightly golden. Transfer the cookies to cooling racks and allow to fully cool.

Make the royal icing:

1. Combine the confectioner's sugar and meringue powder in a large bowl. Add the water and beat for 7 minutes, until it is smooth and when drizzled, stays on the surface for a few seconds.

2. Place the icing into a piping bag fitted with a small, round piping tip.

To decorate:

1. Pipe the outline of the fish and fill it in with icing. Allow this to thoroughly dry, about 4 to 5 hours.

2. Use the edible ink pens to draw the stripes and details onto the cookies. Allow the ink to dry and you're done!

CRAB WHOOPIE PIES

MAKES 10-15 WHOOPIE PIES

Whoopie pies are so much fun to make and even better when they taste like red velvet! We're filling them with the most delicious cream cheese filling you'll ever taste. I even make these JUST for the filling sometimes. It is so wonderfully creamy, light, and smooth—I can't wait for you to try it!

Batter:
2 cups all-purpose flour
2 Tbsp. cocoa powder
½ tsp. baking powder
¼ tsp. salt
½ cup unsalted butter, room temperature
1 cup brown sugar
1 large egg
1 tsp. vanilla extract
½ cup buttermilk
1 oz red food coloring

Filling:
1½ cups + 2 Tbsp. unsalted butter, room temperature
8 oz cream cheese, room temperature
1 tsp. vanilla extract
2¼ cups confectioner's sugar
Red candy melts, melted
Candy eyes

Make the batter:
1. Preheat oven to 350°F. Prepare a baking sheet lined with parchment paper.

2. Combine the flour, cocoa powder, baking powder, and salt in a bowl.

3. In a separate bowl, beat the butter and brown sugar with an electric mixer until pale and fluffy. Add the egg and vanilla and mix well. Add the flour mixture in 3 additions, alternating with the buttermilk.

Then add the red food coloring and mix until just combined.

4. Dollop tablespoon-sized pieces of batter onto your prepared sheets and bake for 5 to 8 minutes. Cool them on the pan for 10 minutes, then transfer to a wire rack and cool completely.

Make the filling:
1. Beat the butter and cream cheese with an electric mixer until fluffy. Add the vanilla extract and combine. Add the confectioner's sugar and beat until light and fluffy.

Assembly:
1. Use the red candy melts to draw the claws and legs onto a flat tray lined with parchment paper. Place in the freezer to allow the candy melts to set.

2. Place the filling into a piping bag fitted with a large, round tip and pipe onto half of the cakes. Place another cake on top, then stick the legs and claws into the filling. Use a small amount of filling to attach candy eyes. Enjoy!

This recipe has a video tutorial! Check out my pankobunny YouTube channel to see how to make it.

Peach Sandcastle Doughnuts

MAKES 15-18 DOUGHNUTS

These doughnuts have fresh peaches in them and taste so deliciously juicy and fresh. They are lightly brushed with peach syrup, then dunked in cinnamon sugar, and let me tell you—you will never want any other doughnut again. These are so amazing!

Doughnuts:
½ cup unsalted butter, room temperature
1 cup sugar
3 eggs, room temperature
1½ cups + 1 Tbsp. flour
½ tsp. baking soda
½ tsp. salt
½ cup + 2 Tbsp. sour cream
3–4 peaches, finely diced
¾ tsp. vanilla extract
¾ Tbsp. peach jam

Topping:
¼ cup peach jam
¼ cup water
¼ cup sugar
1¼ tsp. cinnamon
Mini marshmallows
Toothpicks, cut in half
Washi tape
¼ cup white chocolate chips, melted
Pink and purple oil-based food coloring
Brown sugar

Directions:

1. Preheat oven to 350°F. Grease and flour a doughnut pan.

2. Place the butter and sugar in a bowl and beat with an electric mixer until pale and fluffy. Add the eggs one at a time, mixing with each addition.

3. In a separate bowl, mix together 1½ cups of flour, baking soda, and salt. Add this to the butter mixture in 2 additions, alternating with sour cream. Mix the peaches with 1 tablespoon flour and add to the batter, along with the vanilla extract and ¾ tablespoon peach jam.

4. Pour the batter into your prepared pan and tap several times to remove any air bubbles. Bake the doughnuts for 15 to 20 minutes. Let the doughnuts cool in the pan for 15 minutes, then remove them from the pan and transfer to a cooling rack and fully cool.

5. Combine ¼ cup peach jam with ¼ cup water. In a separate bowl, combine the sugar and cinnamon. Working with one doughnut at a time, brush each with the peach jam glaze. Then dunk into the cinnamon and sugar. Skewer mini marshmallows onto toothpicks and brush with the jam glaze, then coat in cinnamon sugar and stick them into the doughnuts to create sandcastles. Stick some washi tape onto a toothpick and stick it into the top of each sandcastle to look like a flag.

6. Divide the melted white chocolate into two bowls and dye them coral and light purple. Spoon the chocolate onto a tray lined with parchment paper and shape them into starfish. Place the tray in the freezer for 5 to 10 minutes until the chocolate is fully set.

7. To serve, sprinkle some brown sugar onto a tray to look like sand, and place the doughnuts on top. Top with the chocolate starfish and enjoy!

This recipe has a video tutorial! Check out my pankobunny *YouTube channel to see how to make it.*

Sand Dollar Shortbread Cookies

MAKES 15-20 COOKIES

This shortbread recipe is so delicately sweet with the perfect touch of salt. If you're looking for a bit of a change from sugar cookies, try this recipe out! These cookies are cute enough for a birthday party, yet elegant enough as a seaside wedding favor.

Ingredients:

1 cup unsalted butter, room temperature
½ cup confectioner's sugar
1 tsp. vanilla extract
2 cups all-purpose flour
¾ tsp. salt
½ cup sliced almonds
½ Tbsp. ground cinnamon

Directions:

1. Beat the butter with an electric mixer until pale and fluffy. Add the confectioner's sugar and beat for 2 minutes, until well combined. Add the vanilla and combine. In a separate bowl, combine the flour and salt, then add to the butter mixture. Mix until the dough sticks together when pinched.

2. Wrap the dough in plastic wrap and refrigerate until firm, about 1 hour.

3. Preheat oven to 325°F. Prepare a baking sheet lined with parchment paper.

4. Roll the dough out on a floured surface to ¼-inch-thick. Use a circle-shaped cookie cutter to cut out rounds and place onto your prepared baking sheet. Press 5 almonds onto each cookie in the shape of a flower.

5. Place the cinnamon in a mesh sieve and lightly dust over the cookies.

6. Refrigerate the cookies until firm, about 30 minutes. Bake for 13 to 15 minutes. Cool on the pan for 10 minutes, then transfer to a wire rack and cool completely. Enjoy!

SEASIDE TARTS

MAKES 12 TARTS

Ganache tarts are one of my favorite treats. They are so simple, but taste so luxurious! These little tarts look just like the beach and taste of sweet sugar cookies and white chocolate.

Ingredients:

Cookie dough (recipe from Mermaid Sugar
    Cookies, page 63)
Cooking spray
3 cups good quality white chocolate, melted
1 cup whipping cream, heated until hot
Pinch of salt
Blue food coloring
Gold sprinkles
Rainbow sprinkles

Directions:

1. Roll the dough out on a floured surface to ¼-inch thick. Cut it into 12 rough squares.

2. Spray a square-shaped muffin tin with cooking spray and press the squares into the pan. Trim any uneven edges. Place the pan in the freezer for 30 minutes.

3. Bake at 350°F for 10 to 15 minutes, until the edges are starting to brown. Allow the tarts to cool in the pan. Very gently remove them from the pan and set aside.

4. In a bowl, combine the melted chocolate, whipping cream, salt, and a drop of blue food coloring. Chill in the fridge until it has slightly thickened, then pour it into the tarts.

5. Place the tarts in the fridge until the ganache has fully set, about 2 hours.

6. Decorate with gold sprinkles to look like sand and some rainbow sprinkles.

Mermaid Sugar Cookies

MAKES 10-12 COOKIES

This is my favorite sugar cookie recipe! They are gently sweet, delicious, and perfect for decorating with royal icing! If you'd like to glam up your cookies, use the luster dust technique from my Chocolate Mermaid Tails (page 109) to create metallic hair and tails!

Cookie Dough:
2 cups all-purpose flour
¼ tsp. salt
½ tsp. baking powder
½ cup unsalted butter, room temperature
1 cup sugar
2 Tbsp. milk
1 egg
¾ tsp. vanilla extract
1 tsp. fresh lemon zest

Royal Icing:
1 lb confectioner's sugar
5 Tbsp. meringue powder
¼ cup cold water
Food coloring
Edible ink pens

Bake the cookies:
1. Mix together the flour, salt, and baking powder in a bowl. In a separate bowl, cream the butter and sugar with an electric mixer until it becomes light and fluffy. Add the milk, egg, vanilla, and lemon zest, and mix well. Then slowly add the flour mixture until it is just combined.

2. Shape the dough into a ball, wrap it in plastic wrap, and place in the refrigerator for 1 hour.

3. Preheat oven to 350°F. Prepare a baking sheet lined with parchment paper. Lightly dust some flour onto your countertop, and roll the dough out until it is ¼-inch thick. Use a mermaid-shaped cookie cutter to cut out cookies. Place them on your prepared baking sheet, and bake for about 10 minutes, until lightly golden. Transfer the cookies to cooling racks and allow to fully cool.

Make the royal icing:
1. Combine the confectioner's sugar and meringue powder in a large bowl. Add the water and beat for 7 minutes, until it is smooth and when drizzled, stays on the surface for a few seconds.

2. Divide the icing into bowls and dye it your desired colors for the skin, tail, hair, and bikini top. Place the icing into piping bags fitted with small, round piping tips.

To decorate:
1. Pipe the outline of the tail and fill it in with icing. Then outline the rest of the body and fill it in, using the icing for the skin tone. Allow this to dry to the touch, about 1 to 2 hours.

2. Pipe the hair and bikini top and allow these to dry to the touch, 2 to 3 hours.

3. Draw the facial features and any other desired details with an edible ink pen. Enjoy!

STARFISH SHORTBREAD

MAKES 20-25 COOKIES

Starfish are such pretty creatures and these cookies are no different! We're using a cool technique to give them life-like positions and make them look like they're walking across the seabed!

Ingredients:
1 cup unsalted butter, room temperature
½ cup confectioner's sugar
1 tsp. vanilla extract
2 cups all-purpose flour
¾ tsp. salt
Aluminum foil
1 egg white, beaten
Orange food coloring
¼ cup orange-colored sugar

Directions:
1. Beat the butter with an electric mixer until pale and fluffy. Add the confectioner's sugar and beat for 2 minutes, until well combined. Add the vanilla and combine. In a separate bowl, combine the flour and salt, then add to the butter mixture. Mix until the dough sticks together when pinched.

2. Wrap the dough in plastic wrap and refrigerate until firm, about 1 hour.

3. Roll the dough out on a floured surface to ¼-inch thick. Use a star-shaped cookie cutter to cut out star cookies. Place them on a baking sheet lined with parchment paper. Use aluminum foil to roll up little balls and misshapen logs, and place them under the stars in various positions. This will make it look like the starfish are walking. Place the entire baking sheet in the freezer for 30 minutes.

4. Preheat oven to 325°F. Add a few drops of orange food coloring to the egg whites and brush them onto the cookies. This will act as an edible "paint." Sprinkle the orange sugar over the surface.

5. Bake for 13 to 15 minutes. Cool on the pan completely. Gently remove the foil from the cookies—they are delicate, so be careful! Enjoy!

DRINKS

Shark Ice Cream Float

MAKES 1

The most delicious way to swim with the sharks! I love ice cream floats and this is the cutest, most summery way to enjoy them!

Ingredients:
Blue Hawaiian punch juice
Lemon–lime soda
Vanilla ice cream
Shark gummies

Directions:
1. Pour some Hawaiian punch ⅔ of the way into any desired glasses. Top up with some lemon-lime soda until the glasses are almost full.

2. Add a scoop of vanilla ice cream on top and top with some gummy sharks and watch them swim!

This recipe has a video tutorial! Check out my pankobunny *YouTube channel to see how to make it.*

Ocean Water Cocktail

SERVES 4-6

If only actual ocean water tasted this good! For a non-alcoholic version, simply substitute the tequila and curacao with a clear or blue fruit punch of your choice, and taste test while gradually adding the fresh lime juice.

Ingredients:
12 oz clear tequila
8 oz blue curacao
10 oz fresh lime juice
12 oz lemon-lime soda
Ice (optional)

Directions:
1. Combine all ingredients in a pitcher. Add ice, if desired.

2. Pour into your desired glasses. Enjoy!

Pirate's Grog

SERVES 3-4

Ahoy matey! This drink packs a punch! The warmth of the dark rum pairs so deliciously with the lime juice and sugar syrup. For a non-alcoholic version, use cola instead of rum!

Sugar Syrup:
1 cup brown sugar, or demerara sugar
1 cup water
6 oz dark rum
2 oz lime juice
2½ oz sugar syrup
3 oz water

Make the sugar syrup:
1. Place the sugar and water in a small pot and set to high heat. Bring to a boil, then reduce the heat to low and simmer, while stirring, until the sugar has dissolved, about 2 minutes.

2. Remove the pot from the heat immediately and allow to cool completely.

Make the grog:
1. Combine the rum, lime juice, syrup, and water in a pitcher.

2. Serve the grog in bottles for an extra piratey touch!

Mermaid Hot Chocolate

SERVES 2-3

Hot chocolate is a classic and I love this fun twist on it! The white chocolate can be substituted with milk or dark chocolate, but I can't resist the beautiful blue seafoam-like color. Decorate it with "sand" sprinkles to create an island of sweets and whipped cream sitting atop a creamy, milky ocean.

Ingredients:
1 cup milk
1 cup whipping cream (or milk,
   for a thinner consistency)
5 oz good quality white chocolate
Blue food coloring
Whipped cream
Gold sprinkles or brown sugar, for sand
Colorful sprinkles
Chocolate Mermaid Tails (page 109)

Directions:
1. Pour the milk, cream, and chocolate into a pot and set to medium heat. Stir constantly until the chocolate has melted and is fully incorporated.

2. Add a small drop of blue food coloring to dye the hot chocolate pale blue.

3. Pour the hot chocolate into mugs and top with some whipped cream. Decorate with gold sprinkles to look like sand, some colorful sprinkles, and a Mermaid Chocolate Tail.

Messages in a Bottle

MAKES 6-8 SCROLLS

These are a fun addition to any drink at a mermaid- or pirate-themed party! Just pop them into a tall glass (I love these mini milk bottles I found online!) and top with your favorite clear drink. These can be made a couple days in advance. Just make sure to store them in a sealed plastic container in the fridge.

Ingredients:
½ cup cold water
¼ cup powdered gelatin
½ can (8 oz) sweetened condensed milk
Cooking spray
6–8 ring-shaped gummies

Directions:

1. Pour the water and gelatin into a pot and let sit for 10 minutes, until the gelatin has developed.

2. Set the pot to medium-high heat and whisk until the gelatin has dissolved. Add the condensed milk and whisk until fully combined.

3. Spray a large baking sheet with cooking spray and wipe the excess off with a paper towel. Pour the mixture onto the baking sheet and place in the fridge for 30 minutes, until set. It will be very thin and maybe slightly see-through.

4. Use a sharp knife to cut the jelly into rectangles. Roll them into scrolls and stretch a gummy ring onto each scroll.

5. Place these into glass bottles and top with your favorite clear drink!

MERMAID MILKSHAKE

SERVES 2

This is the creamiest milkshake you'll ever have! I love to use classic vanilla ice cream, but you are welcome to experiment with any flavor ice cream, as long as it is pale enough to be dyed blue. This milkshake is thick enough that you'll need a big straw, but not so thick that it'll give you a headache trying to drink it! For a thicker or thinner consistency, simply add more or less milk.

Topping:
2 cups whipping cream
1 tsp. vanilla extract
2 Tbsp. confectioner's sugar
Purple food coloring
Chocolate Seashell Truffles (page 87)
Chocolate Mermaid Tails (page 109)

Milkshake:
2½ cups vanilla ice cream
1 cup milk
1 tsp. vanilla extract
Blue food coloring

Make the topping:
1. Beat the whipping cream with an electric mixer until soft peaks form. Add the vanilla extract, confectioner's sugar, and a drop of purple food coloring and beat until stiff peaks form. Be sure not to over-whip!

2. Place the whipped cream in the fridge while you make the milkshake.

Make the milkshake:
1. Place the ice cream, milk, vanilla extract, and a small drop of blue food coloring into a blender and pulse until smooth.

2. Pour the milkshake into tall glasses.

3. Place the freshly whipped cream into a piping bag or a zip-top bag and snip off the tip, creating a large, round tip.

4. Pipe a swirl of cream on top of each milkshake and garnish with a seashell truffle and mermaid tail.

This recipe has a video tutorial! Check out my pankobunny *YouTube channel to see how to make it.*

SWEETS & TREATS

Mermaid Toast

MAKES 1

Mermaid toast is one of the core recipes of the Mermaid Food trend and it's so easy to see why! It is so beautiful and swirly and quite easy to make. Treat yourself to a glamorous breakfast full of mermaid swirls and gold leaf. You deserve it!

Ingredients:
Toast
Cream cheese
Liquid chlorophyll
Edible gold leaf

Directions:

1. Spread a generous layer of cream cheese onto your toast.

2. To make the green pattern, drop 7 to 8 drops of liquid chlorophyll onto the cream cheese and swirl with a knife to create your desired pattern. Garnish with edible gold leaf.

3. Enjoy!

This recipe has a video tutorial! Check out my pankobunny *YouTube channel to see how to make it.*

Shark Fin Pudding

FILLS 2-3 CHAMPAGNE GLASSES

This delicious layered coconut pudding looks adorable with a little chocolate shark fin sitting on top! I used champagne glasses, but this would be just as cute served in a bowl, or with vanilla cake placed between each layer, like a trifle!

Ingredients:
½ cup granulated sugar
3 Tbsp. cornstarch
Pinch salt
2 large egg yolks
½ cup heavy cream
1½ cups coconut cream
½ tsp. vanilla extract
½ tsp. coconut extract
2 Tbsp. unsalted butter
Blue food coloring
Black candy melts, melted
Whipped cream

Directions:
1. Pour the sugar, cornstarch, and salt into a pot. Whisk to combine. Add the egg yolks and heavy cream and whisk until well combined. Add the coconut cream and mix well.

2. Set the pot to medium-high heat and whisk constantly for 5 to 10 minutes, until the mixture has thickened and is bubbling.

3. Pour the pudding through a sieve, then add the vanilla extract, coconut extract, and butter, whisking until well combined.

4. Press a sheet of plastic wrap onto the surface of the pudding and place in the fridge until chilled, about 3 hours.

5. Divide the pudding into 3 bowls. Dye one bowl light blue and one bowl darker blue.

6. Dollop the black candy melts onto a plate lined with parchment paper, and shape to create shark fins. Transfer the plate to the freezer until the candy melts have fully set, about 10 minutes.

7. Place all 3 colors of pudding in piping bags fitted with round tips. Pipe a dark blue layer, light blue layer, then white layer into tall glasses. Top with some whipped cream and a shark fin chocolate. Enjoy!

This recipe has a video tutorial! Check out my pankobunny *YouTube channel to see how to make it.*

CHOCOLATE SEASHELL TRUFFLES

MAKES ABOUT 15 TRUFFLES

Homemade truffles are one of my favorite treats to make. It feels so indulgent to be able to whip them up at home, and filling them with my homemade dulce de leche is the ultimate treat. These are perfect for snacking on their own, or using as decoration on other recipes. Take a flip through this book and you'll see just how many ways they can be used!

Ingredients:
1 can (unopened) condensed milk (or 1 small jar of dulce de leche)
¼ cup colored candy melts
1–2 tsp. shortening
2 cups white candy melts or white chocolate

Directions:
1. Make homemade dulce de leche (optional): Place the unopened can of condensed milk into a large pot and cover with water. Bring to a boil and boil on high for 3 hours. Drain the pot and rinse with cold water, then leave until it comes down to room temperature. Open the can and you'll have the most delicious, homemade dulce de leche! Set aside.

2. Place the colored candy melts in a microwave-safe bowl and heat for 30-second intervals, stirring at each interval until melted. Add ½ to 2 teaspoons shortening to the candy melts and mix until fully combined. This will give the candy melts a thinner consistency and will create that wash of color over the truffles. The more shortening you add, the thinner the candy melts will be.

3. Use a clean paintbrush to brush the melted candy melts onto the insides of a seashell chocolate mold. Place the mold in the fridge to allow the candy melts to set, about 10 minutes.

4. In the meantime, melt the white candy melts in the microwave. Coat the insides of the mold with the white candy melts, but don't fill the molds completely. You can do this with a spoon. Return the mold to the fridge and chill until firm.

5. Place the dulce de leche into a piping bag or zip-top bag and snip off the end to create a small hole. Fill the truffle shells almost to the top with the dulce de leche. Then spoon some more white candy melts on top, sealing the dulce de leche inside.

6. Return the mold to the fridge to chill until fully set, about 30 minutes. If using chocolate instead of candy melts, I recommend placing them in the freezer instead. Store them at room temperature if using candy melts, or in the fridge if using chocolate.

Beachy Rice Cereal Pops

MAKES 12 POPS

This crispy rice cereal recipe will turn anyone into a crispy rice fanatic. I promise you. Adding vanilla extract adds another layer of flavor and will keep you coming back for more! I even snuck a few for breakfast—they are THAT good!

Ingredients:
½ cup margarine or butter
10 cups marshmallows
1 tsp. vanilla extract
12 cups crispy rice cereal
Cooking spray
12 lollipop sticks
3 cups white candy melts
3 cups blue candy melts
Chocolate Seashell Truffles (page 87)
Blue and white sprinkles

Directions:
1. In a microwave-safe bowl, microwave the margarine or butter for 30 to 60 seconds or until melted. Add the marshmallows, mix to combine, then microwave for 1 to 1½ minutes, stopping halfway to stir. Heat until melted and smooth when stirred. Add the vanilla extract and stir to combine.

2. Add the crispy rice cereal and stir until well combined.

3. Spray a 9 x 9-inch baking dish with cooking spray and press the crispy rice cereal firmly into the pan. Wrap in plastic wrap and place in the fridge to chill overnight.

4. Slice any rounded edges off the crispy rice cereal block, then slice it into 12 tall rectangles.

5. Place the white candy melts into a microwave-safe bowl and heat until melted, stirring at each 30-second interval. Stick the lollipop sticks into the candy melts, then into the top of the crispy rice cereal squares. Place the squares into the fridge to allow the candy melts to set, about 10 minutes.

6. Dunk the crispy rice cereal about ¾ of the way into the remaining white candy melts and place on a tray covered with plastic wrap. Place in the fridge for 30 minutes, or until the candy melts have fully hardened.

7. Melt the blue candy melts and dunk the crispy rice cereal into the candy melts one at a time. Keep some of the white candy melts showing, to look like sea foam. While the blue candy melts are still wet, stick a Chocolate Seashell Truffle (page 87) onto the crispy rice cereal and decorate with sprinkles. Return to the tray and repeat with the remaining crispy rice cereal squares. If you find that the decorations are sliding off, wait until the blue candy melts are almost set, but still tacky. This will only take 30 seconds or so, so work quickly.

Mermaid Swirl Fudge

MAKES TWO 9 X 9-INCH PANS

This is one of my signature recipes and it is a showstopper! It might look like plain old fudge, but take a bite and be transformed into a chocolatey world of pillowy, marshmallow sweetness. The white chocolate can be substituted with milk or dark chocolate and the macadamia nuts can also be swapped out with any crunchy ingredient you like!

Ingredients:

4¾ cups white chocolate
1 cup unsalted butter
½ cup clear corn syrup
2 tsp. vanilla extract
½ cup macadamia nuts
Blue food coloring
½ cup macadamia nuts
5 cups mini marshmallows
1¼ cups mermaid-colored candies
   (+ extra for topping)

Directions:

1. Place the white chocolate, butter, and corn syrup in a pot over medium-low heat. Stir consistently until completely melted. Don't worry if the chocolate and butter have separated. They will come together again as they cool.

2. Remove the pot from the heat and stir the mixture with a spatula or a whisk until the chocolate and butter have fully combined. Add the vanilla extract and a drop of blue food coloring and allow to cool slightly.

3. Add the macadamia nuts, mermaid-colored candies, and marshmallows and mix until just combined. Divide the mixture between two 9 x 9-inch square aluminum containers, and sprinkle some extra candies on top. Cover with aluminum foil and place in the freezer until set.

4. Slice the fudge into bite-sized squares, and you're done!

Aquarium Jell-O Cups

FILLS TWO 8-OUNCE GLASSES

These adorable individual aquariums are a staple for beach- or fish-themed parties. I've loved Jell-O cups like these since I was little and think they're the cutest addition to birthday parties. They can be the centerpiece, or act as sweet little accent pieces to the cake!

Ingredients:
1 cup jelly beans
3½ cups lemon–lime soda, or any clear soda
3 Tbsp. cup powdered gelatin
Blue food coloring
1–3 fish gummies

Directions:
1. Pour the jelly beans into two 8 oz glasses. Set aside.

2. Pour the soda into a bowl and sprinkle the gelatin over the surface. Allow the gelatin to develop for 5 minutes. Transfer the gelatin mixture to a pot and set to medium heat. Whisk until the gelatin has fully dissolved.

3. Pour the liquid into a clear or white bowl—anything that will allow you to see the color clearly. Add a very small drop of blue food coloring; enough to ever so slightly tint the liquid blue. If it is too dark, you won't be able to see the fish!

4. Chill the liquid in the fridge until it is halfway set, about 1 hour. Fill the glasses with the jelly and stick some gummy fish inside. The half-set jelly will allow the fish to stay suspended, while keeping the water looking seamless.

5. Place the glasses in the fridge until the jelly has completely set, about 3 to 4 hours. Enjoy!

Mermaid Puppy Chow

SERVES 5-6

Puppy chow is the ideal snacking food—and not actually for puppies! Whip this up for a mermaid-themed sleepover: serve it in little buckets, turn on a movie, and snuggle under some sea blue blankets. This is also great for packing in lunchboxes if you have some left over!

Ingredients:
¼ cup semi-sweet chocolate chips
½ cup dulce de leche caramel
Large pinch of salt
2 Tbsp. unsalted butter
4½ cups Chex™ cereal
1½ cups confectioner's sugar
1 cup shark gummies
1 cup pink, blue, purple, and green Jujubes™
   or other gummy candy

Directions:
1. Combine the chocolate chips, dulce de leche caramel, salt, and butter and microwave for 30 seconds until melted.

2. Pour on top of the Chex™ cereal, stirring until the cereal is well coated. Pour the puppy chow into a large resealable bag and add the powdered sugar. Shake until well coated.

3. Pour the puppy chow onto a baking sheet to cool. Add the shark gummies and Jujubes™.

4. Once it has fully cooled, pour the puppy chow into a bowl and enjoy!

Edible Sand

SERVING SIZE WILL DEPEND ON HOW MANY CAKE SCRAPS YOU USE!

A necessity at a mermaid party! Brown sugar is a popular option for edible sand, but sometimes it can be too much additional sugar. This sand is made from excess cake scraps that can be taken from offcuts of a cake or from a few spare cupcakes. As you'll see in this book, it is great for use as a topping in the Sandcastle Cake (page 45) or as an accent on a dessert platter.

Ingredients:
Vanilla or lemon cake scraps

Directions:

1. Crumble the cake into small pieces. Scatter onto a baking sheet lined with parchment paper.

2. Set the oven to 250°F and dry the crumbs for 20 to 30 minutes, until dry. Cool completely.

3. Place the crumbs into a food processor and pulse until they resemble sand.

4. Use in your favorite beachy recipe!

CANDY SEAWEED

SERVING WILL VARY DEPENDING ON HOW MANY CANDY BELTS YOU USE. ABOUT 14 PIECES FOR A GENEROUS SEAWEED BOUQUET.

This cute and easy technique is a great way to add edible décor to your mermaid party. Fill tall glasses with rice or blue candy, then arrange the seaweed on top. They would also be an adorable centerpiece on a cake!

Ingredients:
Green, red, or blue sour candy belts
Bamboo skewers

Directions:
1. Skewer the candy belts onto the bamboo skewers by creating small wave patterns back and forth. For a varied look, twist the candy before each time you skewer it, for an even wavier effect.

2. Stick the skewers into a tall glass or a cake to create a beautiful and delicious sea of seaweed.

Edible Sea Glass

MAKES 4 CUPS SEA GLASS

This is my favorite lollipop recipe that I've repurposed as sea glass! For pale sea glass, use the tiniest amount of food coloring, as a little can go a long way. The sugar has a slightly yellow cast to it before coloring, so keep that in mind when choosing your color.

Ingredients:
1¼ cups granulated sugar
½ cup water
¾ cup light corn syrup
Blue or teal gel food coloring
Cooking spray

Directions:

1. Line a baking sheet with parchment paper, or a silpat mat. If using parchment paper, spray the paper generously with cooking spray. Set aside.

2. Place a pot over medium heat, and add the granulated sugar, water, and light corn syrup. Stir with a rubber spatula until everything is melted and combined.

3. Increase the heat to medium-high, and attach a candy thermometer to the pot. Heat the sugar until it reaches 300°F, stirring occasionally. Add a small drop of the blue or teal food coloring and mix well. When the mixture reaches 310°F, remove from the heat and mix until it stops bubbling.

4. Pour the mixture onto the baking sheet and allow the candy to cool completely.

5. Smash the candy into smaller pieces with your hands, a small hammer, or the back of a spoon. It might be sharp, so be careful! Transfer the candy to a resealable bag and toss it a few times, to dull any edges and give the candy the soft, smooth look of sea glass.

6. Pour into your desired dish and enjoy!

MALIBU MERMAID PANNA COTTA

FILLS SIX 8-OUNCE GLASSES

Panna cotta is one of my favorite desserts. It is so smooth and creamy and this particular recipe has been personally approved by my Italian loved ones. It is legit and it is delicious! We are using a fun technique to create these graphic color-blocked angles, which brings me right back to the nineties!

Ingredients:

6 Tbsp. water
4 tsp. powdered gelatin
3 cups whipping cream
¾ cup granulated sugar
1 cup milk
1 tsp. vanilla extract
Pink, green, blue, and purple food coloring
Whipped cream
Sprinkles

Directions:

1. Pour the water into a bowl and sprinkle the gelatin on top. Allow the gelatin to develop for 5 minutes.

2. Pour the whipping cream and sugar into a pot and set to medium-high heat. Whisk until the sugar has fully dissolved and heat until bubbles begin to form at the edges, about 2 minutes. Remove the pan from the heat and add the gelatin. Whisk until the gelatin has fully dissolved.

3. Pour the liquid through a sieve into a large bowl. The sieve will catch any pieces of undissolved gelatin. Add the milk and vanilla extract and whisk to combine.

4. Divide the mixture between 4 bowls. Dye one each pink, green, blue, and purple.

5. Place the glasses into a baking dish that fits into your fridge. Use a dishtowel to prop up and sit the glasses at an angle. Pour ⅙ of one color into each glass, being careful not to splash it all over the glass. I used a spoon to carefully pour it in. Place the entire baking dish in the fridge and chill for 2 to 3 hours, until the panna cotta is firm to the touch and the glass can be rotated the opposite way without the panna cotta sliding or breaking.

6. Place the glasses at an angle opposite to how they were and pour ⅙ of another color into each glass. Return to the fridge and chill for 2 to 3 more hours. Repeat with the other 2 colors, rotating the glass each time. For the final layer, sit the glasses upright, so that the surface of the panna cotta will be flat. While you are waiting for each layer to set, the remaining unused panna cotta can be covered with plastic wrap and kept at room temperature. If it starts to set, give it a little stir and it should be easy to pour.

7. Once all layers have been poured, chill the panna cotta overnight. When ready to serve, top with some whipped cream and sprinkles. This version of panna cotta stays in the glass, so no need to worry about unmolding it!

Reef Mallows

MAKES 14 POPS

If you make one recipe in this book, let it be this! These little coral reefs taste like chocolate bars on a stick. The salted peanuts and sweet, homemade caramel are the most delicious combination and taste heavenly with the light, fluffy marshmallow filling.

Ingredients:
14 jumbo marshmallows
14 lollipop sticks
2½ cups soft caramel candies
2 Tbsp. milk
2 cups salted peanuts
2 cups blue candy melts
Fish and rainbow sprinkles

Directions:
1. Stick a lollipop stick into each marshmallow and arrange on a baking sheet lined with parchment paper.

2. Place the caramels and milk in a pot and set to medium heat. Keep stirring until the candies have fully melted.

3. Remove the pot from the heat. Working with one marshmallow at a time, dunk the marshmallow into the caramel and fully coat all sides. Allow the excess caramel to drip off, then immediately roll the marshmallow into the peanuts, sticking peanuts to all sides.

4. Place the marshmallow onto the parchment paper-lined baking sheet and gently press the peanuts into the caramel, to ensure they are secure.

5. Repeat with the remaining marshmallows. Place the baking sheet in the fridge to chill until the marshmallows and caramel have stiffened.

6. Melt the candy melts in a microwave-safe bowl for 30-second intervals, until fully melted. Working with one marshmallow at a time, dunk the marshmallow into the chocolate, coating all sides. Tap the lollipop stick on the edge of the bowl to remove any excess candy melts, then decorate with the fish and rainbow sprinkles. The cool temperature of the chilled marshmallows will cause the candy melts to set relatively quickly, so make sure to attach any sprinkles while the candy melts are still tacky.

7. Return the marshmallow to the baking sheet and repeat with the remaining marshmallows. Chill the marshmallows in the fridge to set the candy melts, then enjoy!

Beachy Chocolate-Covered Oreos

MAKES 6 COOKIES

Chocolate-covered Oreos™ are super trendy nowadays, so I thought up a cute, beachy twist! These are great party favors and make great leftovers for snacking with a movie!

Ingredients:
3 cups blue candy melts
6 Oreo™ cookies
1 cup white candy melts
Silver and gold luster dust
1 Tbsp. vodka

Directions:

1. Place the blue candy melts in a microwave-safe bowl and microwave for 30-second intervals, until fully melted.

2. Place a dollop of blue candy melts into each cavity of an Oreo™ mold. Tap the mold on your work surface a couple times to spread the candy melts over the entire base of each cavity. Place an Oreo™ into each cavity and fill them the rest of the way with blue candy melts. Tap the mold on your work surface again to smooth the surface. Place the mold in the fridge for the candy melts to stiffen, about 45 minutes. (If you don't have an Oreo™ mold, you can simply dunk the cookies into a bowl of candy melts.)

3. In the meantime, make the sand dollar accents (you could also try pairing this with the Sand Dollar Shortbread on page 59!). Melt the white candy melts in a microwave-safe bowl, stirring at 30-second intervals. Pour the candy melts into a sand dollar-shaped chocolate mold and place in the fridge until the candy melts have fully set, about 20 minutes. Unmold and set on a plate.

4. In a small bowl, combine equal parts silver and gold luster dust. Add enough vodka to create a liquid with a similar consistency to maple syrup or paint. Use a clean paintbrush to paint the luster dust paint onto the sand dollars. Paint 2 to 3 coats, allowing a few minutes between each coat for the last coat to dry.

5. Unmold the chocolate-covered Oreos™. Place a dollop of white candy melts on top and stick a sand dollar on top. Serve and enjoy!

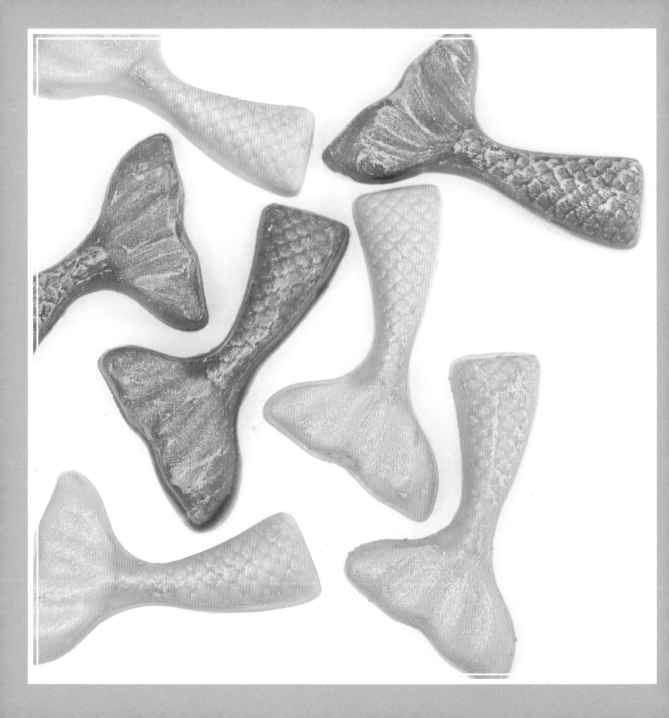

CHOCOLATE MERMAID TAILS

1 CUP CANDY MELTS MAKES 6-7 TAILS

These mermaid tails are the center of the mermaid trend, so I absolutely had to include them! These are perfect to serve as is, or used as decoration to mermaid-ify any dessert of your choice. Stick them onto a cake, cupcakes, or even ice cream!

Ingredients:
Candy melts
Gold luster dust (optional)
1 Tbsp. vodka (for luster dust)

Directions:

1. Place the candy melts in a microwave-safe bowl and heat for 30-second intervals, stirring at each interval, until melted.

2. Pour into a mermaid tail-shaped chocolate mold and tap the mold on your work surface a couple times to smooth the surface. Place the mold in the fridge for 30 minutes, or until the candy melts have set.

3. If desired, add a golden sheen to the tails. Combine the gold luster dust and a couple drops of vodka in a small dish, until it is the consistency of paint or maple syrup. Use a clean paintbrush to paint it onto the tails. Allow it to dry and enjoy!

Mermaid Ice Cream

MAKES 1 QUART

This is my favorite no-churn ice cream recipe! It is so easy to whip up and is amazingly creamy and delicious. For an extra mermaid-y effect, top with some whipped cream, a Chocolate Mermaid Tail, and some colorful sprinkles!

Ingredients:
2 cups whipping cream
1 can (14 oz) condensed milk
1 tsp. vanilla extract
Pink, green, blue, and purple food coloring

Directions:

1. Beat the whipping cream with an electric mixer until stiff peaks form.

2. In a separate bowl, combine the condensed milk and vanilla extract. Add a large dollop of whipped cream and mix until combined. Add the remaining whipped cream and gently fold until combined.

3. Divide the mixture into 4 bowls. Dye the bowls pink, green, blue, and purple.

4. Spoon alternating dollops of each color into a plastic container. I recommend using a clear container, so that you can see the pattern from the outside!

5. Seal the container closed, then freeze for 6 hours, or until stiff. Enjoy!

CRISPY MERMAID TAIL WITH BARNACLES

MAKES A 15-INCH TALL TAIL

If you are looking for an alternative to a cake, this is the perfect centerpiece! To eat, simply cut slices with a sharp knife.

Ingredients:
½ cup margarine or butter
10 cups marshmallows
1 tsp. vanilla extract
Green food coloring
12 cups crispy rice cereal
Cooking spray
2–3 lollipop sticks or bamboo skewers
2 cups buttercream (see Coral Reef Cupcakes recipe, page 25)
Chocolate Seashell Truffles (page 87)
Pink and white sprinkles

Directions:

1. In a microwave-safe bowl, microwave the margarine or butter for 30 to 60 seconds or until melted. Add the marshmallows, mix to combine, then microwave for 1 to 1½ minutes, stopping halfway to stir. Heat until melted and smooth when stirred. Add the vanilla extract and green food coloring and stir to combine.

2. Add the crispy rice cereal and stir until well combined.

3. Cover your work surface with plastic wrap. Spray your hands with cooking spray and shape ¾ of the crispy rice cereal into the body of the tail. Shape the remaining crispy rice cereal into the fin. Wrap both pieces in plastic wrap and chill in the fridge overnight.

4. Unwrap the two pieces and attach them using lollipop sticks. You may need to use a couple to securely attach the fin.

5. Place ⅓ cup of buttercream into a piping bag fitted with a small, star-shaped piping tip. Dye the rest of the buttercream green and spread it sparingly over the entire surface of the fin. You want to be able to see the texture of the crispy rice cereal, but also give the fin a clean look and hide any crevices.

6. Stick some Chocolate Seashell Truffles and sprinkles onto the tail, and pipe dollops of white buttercream. This will look like barnacles! Enjoy!

TURTLE TRUFFLES

MAKES 6-10 TRUFFLES

These little sea turtles are the perfect little snack or addition to your mermaid dessert spread! Package these in little cellophane bags as take-home party favors and put a smile on your guests' faces!

Ingredients:
¼ cup brown candy melts
½ tsp. shortening
2 cups green candy melts
1½ cups good quality milk chocolate, melted
½ cup whipping cream, heated until hot
Pinch of salt

Directions:
1. Place the brown candy melts in a microwave-safe bowl and microwave for 30 second intervals, stirring at each interval, until melted. Add the shortening and mix until melted.

2. Use a clean paintbrush to paint the shell portion of a turtle-shaped chocolate mold. Place the mold in the fridge to chill.

3. Place the green candy melts in a microwave-safe bowl and microwave for 30 second intervals, stirring at each interval, until melted. Coat the insides of the turtle mold with the candy melts, but don't fill the mold, then return it to the fridge to chill.

4. In a bowl, combine the milk chocolate, whipping cream, and pinch of salt. Pour it into the chocolate shells, leaving a little bit of space at the top. Place the mold in the fridge until the ganache is very firm, about 1 hour. Pour more green candy melts on top to seal the truffles closed and chill for an additional 30 minutes.

5. Unmold the turtles and enjoy!

Mermaid Hot Chocolate Spoons

MAKES 6 SPOONS

These spoons are a fun snack or perfect as a party favor! Place them in a cellophane bag and send them home with guests, or save them for cozy days at home. They are simple, delicious, and can be made days in advance!

Ingredients:
2 cups candy melts, any color
¼ cup sprinkles in a variety of shapes, sizes, and colors

Directions:

1. Place each color of candy melts into their own microwave-safe bowl and microwave for 30-second intervals, stirring at each interval, until melted.

2. Pour the candy melts into a spoon-shaped silicone mold. Place the mold in the fridge until the candy melts have set, about 20 minutes.

3. Unmold the spoons. Working with one spoon at a time, dip the end of the spoon into more melted candy melts. Immediately dunk it into the sprinkles. Place on a plate lined with plastic wrap and continue with the rest of the spoons.

4. Chill the spoons in the fridge for a final 20 minutes, then enjoy!

Fish Pond Jellies

SERVES 6

This is one of my oldest recipes, but I still love it! This is a form of Japanese Wagashi, traditional Japanese sweets. Beans are commonly used in desserts in Japan, so don't be too scared! These beautiful little jellies look like floating ponds and pair wonderfully with some green tea.

Fish:
½ cup milk
½ cup water
1 tsp. powdered agar
Red food coloring

Base of the pond:
1 cup water
1 tsp. powdered agar
1 tsp. sugar
½ tsp. matcha powder
1 small can cooked mixed beans, drained
    and rinsed (like white beans and red
    kidney beans)

Pond "water":
2¼ cups water
3 tsp. powdered agar
3 cups sugar
1½ Tbsp. clear corn syrup
4½ Tbsp. clear ume shu (plum wine)

To make the fish:
1. Pour the water, milk, and powdered agar into a small pot, and mix together, dissolving the agar-agar. Bring to a boil, and then bring it down to low heat and simmer for 1 to 2 minutes. Turn off the heat, and allow it to slightly cool in the pot.

2. Divide the mixture into 2 small containers. Color one half of the milk red with food coloring. Drop small droplets of the red milk into the white milk and gently swirl it around to create a marble effect.

3. Place the container in the fridge until the jelly is fully set, then remove the jelly from the container and cut it into fish shapes using a knife or small cookie cutter.

To make the base of the pond:
1. Pour the water and agar-agar into a pot, and mix together. Set to high, and dissolve the agar-agar as the water heats up. When it reaches a boil, bring the heat down to low and simmer for 3 to 4 minutes. After simmering, add and completely dissolve the sugar and matcha powder.

2. Pour the majority of the jelly into a 7 x 4-inch container. Pour the remaining 2 tablespoons or so into a small dish. Place both dishes into the fridge until fully set.

3. Keep the larger amount of jelly in the dish, but remove the jelly from the small dish. Slice it into leaves and lily pads and set aside. Make small, shallow slices

continued on next page

across the entire surface. This creates a bit of texture, so that the pond water has something to grip to when we pour it on top. Set aside.

To make the pond water:

1. Pour the water and agar-agar into a pot, and mix together. Set to high, and dissolve the agar-agar as the water heats up. When it reaches a boil, bring the heat down to low and simmer for 3 to 4 minutes. After simmering, add and completely dissolve the sugar, corn syrup, and ume shu (plum wine). Allow the jelly to cool for 2 minutes.

2. Pour about ⅓ of the water jelly into the container with the matcha jelly. Arrange the drained and rinsed beans inside the container to look like stones on the bottom of the pond. When the jelly has almost set (3 to 5 minutes), pour in another ⅓ of the jelly. Add the fish and the leaves and lily pads. Once the jelly has almost set (3 to 5 minutes), pour in the remaining jelly. Place the jelly in the fridge until completely set, about 20 minutes.

3. Carefully slide the jelly out of the container, slice into as many slices as desired, and enjoy!

This recipe has a video tutorial! Check out my pankobunny *YouTube channel to see how to make it.*

Acknowledgments

I would like to thank my publisher, Skyhorse Publishing, and my editor, Leah Zarra, for giving me the opportunity to work with them again and write a second cookbook. I am beyond touched and humbled to have been given such a wonderful opportunity and thrilled that I was deemed worthy enough to take a chance on again. I am still pinching myself! Cookbook writing has been a huge goal of mine and I cannot believe that it is already a reality for me.

I am also incredibly grateful to my audience on YouTube, Instagram, and Facebook. This would not have been possible without each and every one of you. Your continuing support, sweet comments, and enthusiasm bring me so much joy and have allowed me to live a life I never dreamed possible. I will always cherish this gift and never forget that it is thanks to all of you.

Lastly, I would like to thank YOU, who picked up this book! I hope that it is everything you hoped it would be, and that I can help to bring some sparkle and underwater goodies into your kitchen.

INDEX

Conversion Charts

METRIC AND IMPERIAL CONVERSIONS

(These conversions are rounded for convenience)

Ingredient	Cups/Tablespoons/Teaspoons	Ounces	Grams/Milliliters
Butter	1 cup/16 tablespoons/2 sticks	8 ounces	230 grams
Cheese, shredded	1 cup	4 ounces	110 grams
Cream cheese	1 tablespoon	0.5 ounce	14.5 grams
Cornstarch	1 tablespoon	0.3 ounce	8 grams
Flour, all-purpose	1 cup/1 tablespoon	4.5 ounces/0.3 ounce	125 grams/8 grams
Flour, whole wheat	1 cup	4 ounces	120 grams
Fruit, dried	1 cup	4 ounces	120 grams
Fruits or veggies, chopped	1 cup	5 to 7 ounces	145 to 200 grams
Fruits or veggies, puréed	1 cup	8.5 ounces	245 grams
Honey, maple syrup, or corn syrup	1 tablespoon	0.75 ounce	20 grams
Liquids: cream, milk, water, or juice	1 cup	8 fluid ounces	240 milliliters
Oats	1 cup	5.5 ounces	150 grams
Salt	1 teaspoon	0.2 ounces	6 grams
Spices: cinnamon, cloves, ginger, or nutmeg (ground)	1 teaspoon	0.2 ounce	5 milliliters
Sugar, brown, firmly packed	1 cup	7 ounces	200 grams
Sugar, white	1 cup/1 tablespoon	7 ounces/0.5 ounce	200 grams/12.5 grams
Vanilla extract	1 teaspoon	0.2 ounce	4 grams

OVEN TEMPERATURES

Fahrenheit	Celsius	Gas Mark
225°	110°	¼
250°	120°	½
275°	140°	1
300°	150°	2
325°	160°	3
350°	180°	4
375°	190°	5
400°	200°	6
425°	220°	7
450°	230°	8